The Ocean
by Michèle Dufresne

Contents

PIONEER VALLEY EDUCATIONAL PRESS

Chapter 1
A Hot Day

It was a very hot day.
Bella and Rosie
were at the beach.

"I'm hot," said Bella.

"Me, too," said Rosie.

"Let's go swimming,"
said Bella.

Bella ran down to the water and jumped in. "Come on, Rosie," she called.

"Oh, no!" said Rosie.
"I'm too afraid
of the water!"

"Come on!" said Bella.
"Come on!
Come and swim with me.
Don't be afraid!"

Bella swam up
and down in the waves.
"Come on!" she called.
"It's nice and cool.
Come on in!"

"No!" said Rosie.
"I'm afraid!"

Bella started to shout.
"Help! Help!
Rosie! Help!"

"Oh, no!" said Rosie.
"Bella needs help!"

Rosie began to swim
to Bella.
"Here I come, Bella.
Here I come to help you."

"Bella, are you OK?"
asked Rosie.

"Yes," said Bella.
"I just wanted you to get
in the water."

"Bella!" said Rosie.
"That was a bad idea!
What if I couldn't swim?
Then I might need help."

"Oh," said Bella.
"I didn't think of that!"

Chapter 2
A Boat Ride

When Bella and Rosie came out of the water, their new friend, Olive, was standing next to a boat.

"Hello, Bella and Rosie!" said Olive. "Look at this boat. Do you want to go for a boat ride?"

"A boat ride?" said Bella.
"That sounds like fun!"

"I am afraid of boats,"
said Rosie.

"Come on, Rosie," said Bella.
"It will be fun!"

Olive jumped into the boat.
"Come on!" she said.

Bella jumped into the boat.

"Oh look! There are bones in the boat!" said Bella.

"Bones!" said Rosie, and she jumped into the boat, too.

Then Rosie looked around.

"Bella!" said Rosie.
"There are no bones
in this boat."

"We don't need bones
to have fun. Let's go
for a ride!" said Olive.

"Here we go!" said Bella.
"Isn't this fun?"

"Bella, you tricked me,
again," said Rosie.
She looked mad.

"I'm sorry," said Bella.
"I wanted you to have fun
with me in the boat!"

18

"It is fun," said Rosie.
"But remember, tricking me
isn't nice."

"I just love the beach,"
said Bella. "I love the sand,
I love the water,
I love the clams,
and I love the boat!"

"Me, too!" said Rosie.
"Me, too!"